GW00514626

an invitation to

CELEBRATE

an invitation to
CELEBRATE

EDITED BY
WYNN WHELDON

MQP

Hear the mellow wedding bells
    Golden bells!
What a world of happiness their
    harmony fortells
Through the balmy air of night
How they ring out their delight!

Edgar Allan Poe

For man, as for flower and beast and bird, the supreme triumph is to be most vividly, most perfectly alive.

D.H. Lawrence

Dignity does not come in possessing honors, but in deserving them.

Aristotle

Boys, baseball is a game
where you gotta have fun.
You do that by winning.

Dave Bristol

I celebrate myself,
   and sing myself,
And what I assume
   you shall assume,
For every atom
   belonging to me as
   good belongs to you.

Walt Whitman

Inches make a champion.

Vince Lombardi

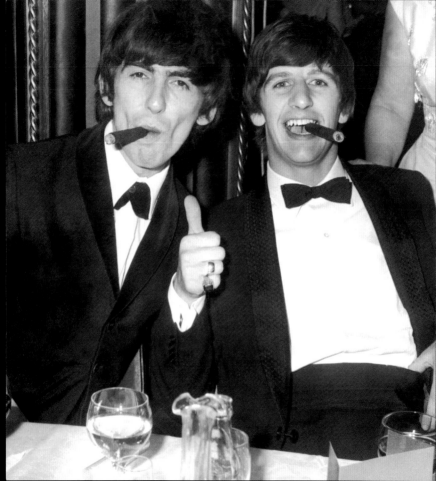

Happy the man, and happy he alone,
He who can call today his own:
He who, secure within, can say,
Tomorrow do thy worst, for I have lived today.

John Dryden

Nothing is worth more than this day.

Johann Wolfgang von Goethe

If you think you can win, you can win.
Faith is necessary to victory.

William Hazlitt

Ring out the old, ring in the new,
Ring happy bells, across the snow:
This year is going, let him go:
Ring out the false, ring in the true.

Alfred Lord Tennyson

See the conquering
hero comes!
Sound the trumpet,
beat the drums!

Thomas Morell

Ah! on Thanksgiving day,
   when from East and from West,
From North and from South,
   come the pilgrim and guest,
When the gray-haired New Englander
   sees round his board
The old broken links of affection restored,
When the care-wearied man seeks
   his mother once more,
And the worn matron smiles
   where the girl smiled before.
What moistens the lip and
   what brightens the eye?
What calls back the past,
   like the rich Pumpkin pie?

John Greenleaf Whittier

Life affords no higher
pleasure than that of
surmounting difficulties,
passing from one step of
success to another,
forming new wishes and
seeing them gratified.

Samuel Johnson

Far away in the sunshine are my highest aspirations. I may not reach them, but I can look up and see their beauty, believe in them, and try to follow where they lead.

Louisa May Alcott

I am convinced that every boy,
in his heart, would rather steal
second base than an automobile.

Justice Thomas Campbell Clark

Heroism is not only in the man, but in the occasion.

Calvin Coolidge

Come, ye young men, come along,
With your music, dance and song;
Bring your lasses in your hands,
For 'tis that which love commands.
Then to the maypole haste away,
For 'tis now a holiday.

Traditional Staines Morris Song

37

Health is the best that Heaven sends;
Next, to be comely to look upon:
Third is riches justly won:
Fourth, to be young among one's friends.

Simonides

The reward of a thing well done is to have done it.

Ralph Waldo Emerson

I think I should have no other mortal wants, if I could always have plenty of music. It seems to infuse strength into my limbs and ideas into my brain. Life seems to go on without effort, when I am filled with music.

George Eliot

In youth, we clothe ourselves
with rainbows, and go as brave
as the zodiac.

Ralph Waldo Emerson

If I'd known I was
gonna live this long,
I'd have taken better
care of myself.

Eubie Blake

The dogs did bark, the children screamed,
Up flew the windows all;
And every soul bawled out, "Well done!"
As loud as he could bawl.

William Cowper

Those who are lifting the world upward and onward are those who encourage more than criticize.

Elizabeth Harrison

Nor is it always in the most distinguished achievements that men's virtues or vices may be best discovered: but very often an action of small note, a short saying, or a jest, shall distinguish a person's real character more than the greatest sieges, or the most important battle.

Plutarch

The year's at the spring
And day's at the morn:
Morning's at seven:
The hill-sides dew-pearled:
The lark's on the wing:
The snail's on the thorn:
God's in his Heaven –
All's right with the world!

Robert Browning

Let us celebrate the
occasion with wine
and sweet words.

Plautus

This is the day which the Lord hath make; we will rejoice and be glad in it.

The Bible, Psalm 118:24

What sunshine is to flowers, smiles are to humanity. These are but trifles, to be sure; but, scattered along life's pathway, the good they do is inconceivable.

Joseph Addison

My lovely living boy,
My hope, my hap,
my love, my life, my joy.

Guillaume de Salluste Du Bartas

I do not so much rejoice that God
hath made me to be a Queen, as to
be a Queen over so thankful a people.

Elizabeth I

The proper behavior all through the holiday season is to be drunk. This drunkenness culminates on New Year's Eve, when you get so drunk you kiss the person you're married to.

P.J. O'Rourke

Hope is a thing with
　feathers
That perches in the soul,
And sings the tune
　without words
And never stops at all.

Emily Dickinson

Today is the first day
of the rest of your
life – celebrate now!

Graffiti

When a virtuous man is raised,
it brings gladness to his friends,
grief to his enemies, and glory
to his posterity.

Ben Jonson

Townfolk know pleasures,
country people joys.

Minna Thomas Antrim

A merry heart
doeth good like
a medicine.

The Bible, Proverbs 17:22

The smallest feline is a masterpiece.

Leonardo da Vinci

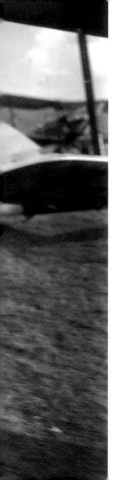

A cloudy day is no match
for a sunny disposition.

William Arthur Ward

My heart leaps up when I behold
A rainbow in the sky:
So was it when my life began;
So is it now I am a man;
So be it when I shall grow old,
Or let me die!
The Child is father of the Man;
I could wish my days to be
Bound each to each by natural piety.

William Wordsworth

Wherever you go,
go with all your heart.

Confucius

Only good girls
keep diaries.
Bad girls don't
have time.

Tallulah Bankhead

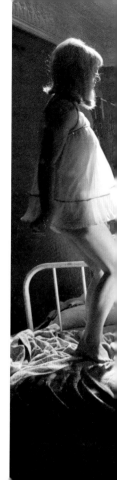

It is not the mountain
we conquer but ourselves.

Sir Edmund Hillary

Watch us bobbing for an apple,
For an apple apple apple,
But no apple apple apple,
Not an apple can I get.

Oh I cannot catch an apple,
Not one apple apple apple,
Though my sister got an apple.
All I got was wet!

On with the dance!
Let joy be unconfined;
No sleep till morn,
   when Youth and Pleasure meet
To chase the glowing Hours
   with flying feet.

Lord Byron

The realization that our small planet is only one of many worlds gives humankind the perspective it needs to realize sooner that our own world belongs to all its creatures, that the moon landing marks the end of our childhood as a race and the beginning of a newer and better civilization.

Sir Arthur C. Clarke

Shall we not then be glad, and rejoice in the joy of our children?

Henry Wadsworth Longfellow

Celebrate the happiness that friends are always giving, make everyday a holiday and celebrate just living!

Amanda Bradley

Think where man's glory
most begins and ends,
And say my glory was I
had such friends.

W. B. Yeats

If the sight of the blue skies fills you with joy, if a blade of grass springing up in the fields has the power to move you, if the simple things of nature have a message that you understand, rejoice, for your soul is alive...

Elenora Duse

… a simultaneous cry of pleasure broke forth from men and women that almost amounted to a shout, and I stood and received the congratulations that thereupon came in.

Sidney Lanier

There was a star danced,
and under that was I born.

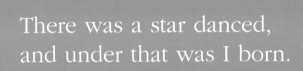

William Shakespeare

The greater the difficulty the more glory in surmounting it.

Epictetus

Picture Credits

All images Hulton Getty Picture Archive, unless otherwise stated.

p.5: Dancer's Marriage, 1971. p.6: The Joy Of Spring, 1946. p.8: Pup Of The Year, 1979. p.1 Great Catch, circa 1955, © Lambert/Archive Photos. p.12: Graduation Day, 1966. p.15: C Tiptoes, circa 1955, © Lambert/Archive Photos. p.16: Thumbs Up From Ringo, 1964, Express Newspapers/Archive Photos p.19: Time For Cake, circa 1955, © Lambert/Archiv Photos. p.21: Elated McEnroe, 1981. p.22 New Year's Eve, 1942, © Archive Photos. p.24: Ne Jump, 1946. p.27: Lunch Time, circa 1945, American Stock/Archive Photos. p.29: Champagn Fountain, 1978. p.30: Two Miss Americas, 1947, © Archive Photos. p.33: Returnin Victorious, circa 1955, Lambert/Archive Photos. p.34: Stripes On The Stars, 1969. p.3 Coronation Maypole, 1953. p.39: Spring Break, circa 1955. p.40: Fish Supper, circa 1955, Lambert/Archive Photos. p.43: Dixieland, 1948. p.45: Girl Graduates. 1933. p.46: Nevc Cockatoo Old, 1956. p.49: Schoolboy Hero, 1935. p.50: Cheerleaders, circa 1950. p.52: Gian Cabbage, 1954. p.54: Skipping Rope, circa 1955, Lambert/Archive Photos. p.57: El Morocc New Year, circa 1935, © Archive Photos. p.59: My Lovely Corn, circa 1955, © Lamber Archive Photos. p.60: Autumn Frolics, 1936. p.63: Come To Daddy, circa 1945, Lamber Archive Photos. p.64: Queen's Coronation, 1953. p.67: A Christmas Kiss, circa 195 Lambert/Archive Photos. p.68: Charity Appeal, 1939. p.71: Wedding Confetti, 1954. p.73: O The Beach, circa 1955, © Archive Photos. p.74: May Fiesta, 1957. p.77: Joie De Vivre, 193 p.78: Top Cat, 1964. p.80: Eureka, 1929. p.83: Royal Fireworks, 1954. p.84: Sack Race, 196 p.87: Pyjama Party, 1965. p.89: At North Pole, 1909. p.90: Apple Bobbing, circa 1945, (Lionel Green/Archive Photos. p.92: The Jive, 1958. p.95: Mission Control, 1969. p.96: On Snowy Hillside, circa 1955, © Lambert/Archive Photos. p.99: Merry Go Round, 1953. p.10 Zoo Party, 1952. p.102: Leap Frog, circa 1935, © Archive Photos. p.105: Tickertape Parad 1969. p.106: Birthday Cake, 1956. p.109: Bannister Record, 1954.

Text Credits

100: Excerpt from "The Municipal Gallery Revisited, VII" by W. B. Yeats, from THE OXFORD DICTIONARY OF QUOTATIONS (Oxford University Press, 1979). Used by permission of A. P. Watt Ltd on behalf of Michael B Yeats.

Published by MQ Publications Limited
12 The Ivories, 6–8 Northampton Street, London N1 2HY
Tel: 020 7359 2244   Fax: 020 7359 1616
mail@mqpublications.com

Copyright © MQ Publications Limited 2002

Design: Bet Ayer
Series Editor: Tracy Hopkins

ISBN: 1 84072 461 7

Printed and bound in China

Cover image © Lambert/Archive Photos.